BARRACUDA
Tiger of the Sea

BARRACUDA
Tiger of the Sea

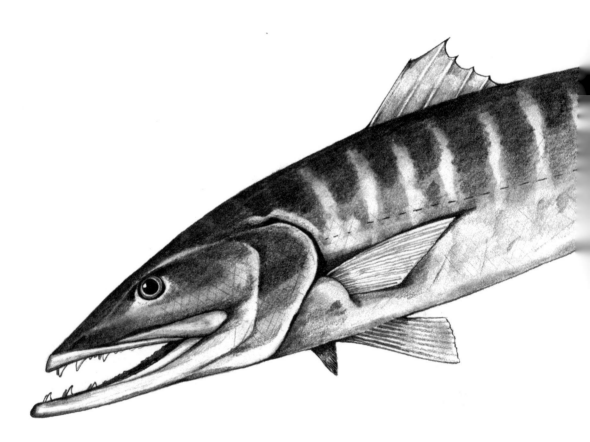

BY FRANCINE JACOBS

ILLUSTRATED BY HARRIETT SPRINGER

 WALKER AND COMPANY
NEW YORK

Library of Congress Cataloging in Publication Data

Jacobs, Francine.
    Barracuda: tiger of the sea.

    Summary: Follows the events of the great barracuda's
life cycle, from hatching to hunting to the laying of eggs.
    1. Great barracuda—Juvenile literature. [1. Great
barracuda. 2. Barracudas]   I. Springer, Harriett.
II. Title.
QL638.S77J32   597'.58   80-54614
ISBN 0-8027-6413-4 (trade)   AACR2
ISBN 0-8027-6414-2 (reinforced)

First published in the United States of America in 1981
by the Walker Publishing Company, Inc.

Published simultaneously in Canada by Beaverbooks,
Limited, Don Mills, Ontario.

Trade ISBN: 0-8027-6413-4
Reinf. ISBN: 0-8027-6414-2

Library of Congress Catalog Card Number: 80-54614

Printed in the United States of America

10 9 8 7 6 5 4 3 2 1

Book designed by Lena Fong Hor

For Albie and Les Salkin

The publisher wishes to thank Professor Donald P. de Sylva, Division of Biology and Living Resources, University of Miami, for reading the text of this book.

It is spring.

The sea shines

under the hot Florida sun.

Waves rise and roll gently.

The ocean looks peaceful,

but danger lies below.

A great barracuda is cruising along.

It is the "tiger of the sea," hunting.

A man in a boat is fishing.

Re-e-e-e! goes his reel.

A jack fish flashes

in the clear, blue water.

The man has the fish on his line.

He winds it in.

The barracuda chases it.

Surprise!

The man pulls up only a fishhead!

The great barracuda has stolen his catch.

The barracuda is on its way

into the open ocean.

Barracudas gather in the deep waters near Florida.

The females lay their eggs in the water.

The males pour their sperm over the eggs.

The sperm enter the eggs and

fertilize them.

This means the eggs can grow into

new barracudas.

Now the parents leave the eggs and

go off alone.

The eggs drift in the water.

Each has a drop of oil that keeps it afloat.

Fish and other sea animals eat many eggs.

The rest of the eggs hatch into tiny barracudas.

The young fish have little sacs of yolk.

They get their food from the yolk.

They cannot swim yet.

They are weak and helpless.

And—in danger!

Big fish eat these small fish.

Those that are left

use up their yolk in a few days.

The baby barracudas are growing.

They are hungry and must eat.

They begin to swim.

They have big eyes.

And sharp teeth.

They catch tiny fish.

Even other little barracudas.

The barracudas look like little twigs
among the plankton—the tiny plants and animals
that float in the sea.
The barracudas keep hunting for food.
Currents and tides slowly take the growing
barracudas toward the land.

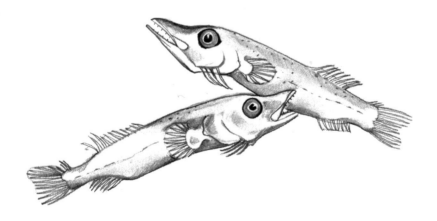

When summer comes,

the barracudas are in warm, shallow waters

close to shore.

They look more like their parents now.

But they are only four inches long.

Their heads are large and pointed.

They have dark eyes and big teeth.

Their bodies are thin and silvery.

The young barracudas need a place

to grow where they are safe from large fish.

A good place is a bed of sea grass
on the sandy bottom near the shore.
Other young animals live here, too.
Fish and shrimp are swimming.
Crabs and spiny lobsters are crawling.

The sea grass hides the young barracudas.
The grass bends and sways with the waves
and so do the barracudas.
Because they hide so well,
they can catch little fish.

23

One day a little barracuda moves away

from the sea grass.

It swims out into deeper water.

A big, hungry fish

sees the young barracuda.

It speeds to catch it.

But before the big fish can get it,

the barracuda dives to the bottom.

The big fish looks and looks.

At last it gives up and swims away.

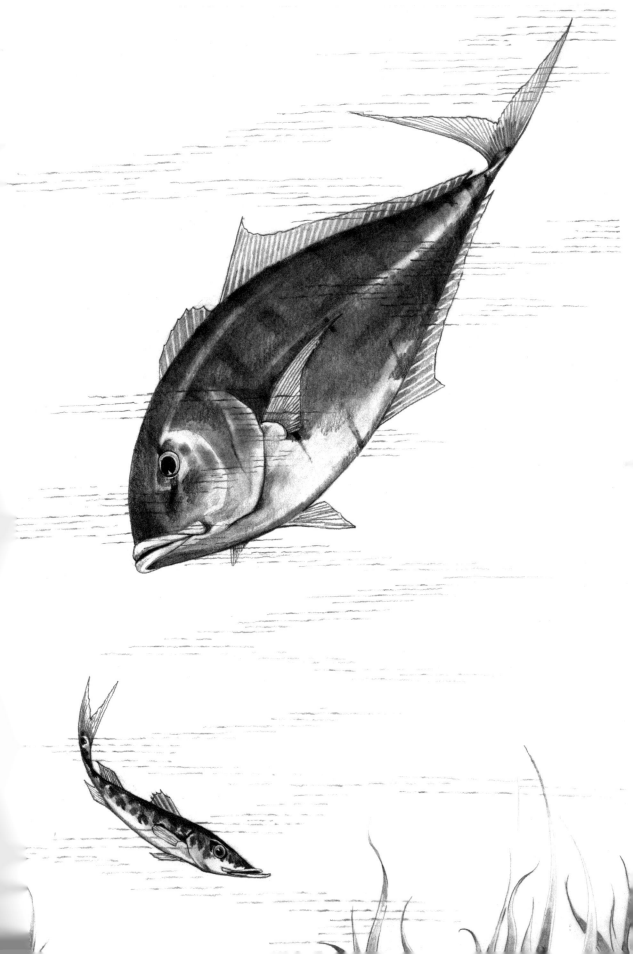

The little barracuda

goes back to the grassy beds.

It is safe.

But not for long.

A fat grouper fish is waiting.

It has a huge mouth.

It comes closer and closer.

The little barracuda flips over

and stands on its head.

It changes color.

Its body now has green bars.

The little barracuda looks like

a blade of grass.

It moves its tail with the moving grass.

The grouper is only inches away.

But it cannot find the barracuda.

It swims on.

The barracuda is safe again.

By the end of the second winter

the barracuda is almost two feet long.

Wherever it goes, the barracuda

makes a place for itself.

It chases away other barracudas.

Fast!

Sometimes the barracuda leaves
its place to catch a passing fish.
Sometimes it leaves and
hunts with other barracudas.
They pounce on schools of sardines
or other small fish.
The little fish scatter.
The barracudas eat the ones
that do not get away fast enough.

34 The barracuda leaves the shore
when it is about three years old.
It travels north along the Florida coasts
in the summer.
It moves back to southern Florida
and the nearby islands in the fall.

The barracuda hunts all the time.
Other fish must watch out
for its long, pale body
with the huge, dark eyes.
They must stay away from
the barracuda's daggerlike teeth
and great, strong jaws.
Few fish can escape the swift barracuda.

The barracuda visits a coral reef.

Small fish swim in and out among the corals.

The barracuda watches the reef fish.

It stays near the surface.

Its silvery body is hidden in the bright light.

It keeps still.

It waits.

The barracuda sees a little grunt fish.

Smack!

The barracuda has its dinner.

After it eats, the barracuda moves along the reef.

It goes to a place where little goby fish wait.

The "tiger of the sea" opens its great mouth.

A tiny goby swims in.

Another meal?

No.

The goby picks at

the barracuda's big teeth.

It gets bits of food to eat.

At the same time

the barracuda gets its teeth cleaned.

One day people come to the coral reef.

They want to see the fish.

The barracuda swims along nearby.

It is very curious.

If the people do not come too close,

the barracuda does not bother them.

But the barracuda can be dangerous.

Once in a great while

a barracuda may attack a swimmer.

This happens when it has trouble seeing.

At sunset.

Or when the sea is not clear.

Or when someone splashes too much.

Barracudas may also attack swimmers

who wear shiny rings, bracelets, or buckles.

They may mistake these bright things

for silvery fish.

The barracuda is an adult
when it is four years old.
But it keeps on growing.
It may grow to five or even six feet
and get to weigh 100 pounds or more.

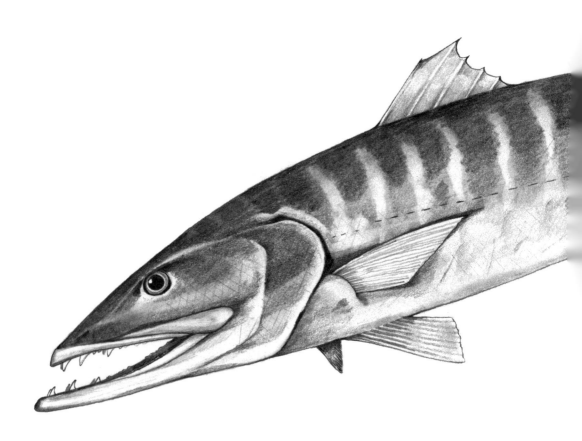

The barracuda might live for twenty years.
Most of its life it travels alone, hunting.

But now it is spring.

And the barracuda joins

other barracudas in the open ocean.

They gather there as their parents did.

Once again eggs and sperm

are poured into the sea.

Once again baby barracudas

start to grow.

The barracuda in this book is the great barracuda *Sphyraena barracuda* found in the warm, tropical waters of all oceans.